Hacking Papers: How to Write a Successful Paper (Even if You Never Did the Reading)

ONE OF AMERICA'S BEST ACADEMIC GHOSTWRITERS SHARES TOP TIPS & STRATEGIES FOR <u>YOUR</u> SUCCESS

Deleuzienne

Published on behalf of Deleuzienne Enterprises

www.Deleuzienne.com

Book Layout ©2018 BookDesignTemplates.com
Cover and author images from iStock via an extended license.

Ordering Information:

Hacking Papers: How to Write a Successful Paper (Even if You Never Did the Reading). Deleuzienne. —1st ed.
ISBN 9781976995590 (paperback)

Contents

Deleuzienne Speaks 8

Research: Work Smarter, Not Harder 10

    A Pairing Menu for Great Source Websites 18

Actually Writing 21

    Bulking Up What You've Got When You've Hit the Wall 25

Putting it all together: Argument & Structure 28

Literally the Worst: Formatting 31

Final Strategies and Useful Resources 34

    Learn from Improv Greats 34

    Read, read, read 36

    Vocabulary 36

    Templates 36

Pep Talk 37

This book is dedicated to my clients. Even the jerks. I truly hope that I helped you achieve your goals.

ACKNOWLEDGEMENTS

I would be remiss if I did not mention the many friends (professors and otherwise) who offered criticism, input, corrections, and innumerable other helpful suggestions for this book. Thanks, guys. I owe you some beer.

Writing is easy. All you have to do is cross out the wrong words.

—Mark Twain

Deleuzienne Speaks

Important Note

If you're in a hurry or facing a looming deadline, skip right ahead to the first chapter. I know your time is precious and I don't want to waste it. Throughout this book, quick tips and summaries will appear in boxes like this one. Onwards!

It's nice to meet you. My name is… unimportant. However, some of you might know me by my pen name, Deleuzienne. Under this name, I have written over *five thousand papers* for students in all subjects, at all levels, and at every type of educational institution you can imagine. Each and every one was an original work. The vast majority of my papers have been well received, and a few times they've missed the mark. Every time, I've learned something new. Over and over, I've seen people stymied or road blocked by common issues, and I've come to believe that many of the people who turn to academic malfeasance to get papers done would not do so if they were empowered with actionable strategies for effectively researching, writing, and editing.

I won't bore you with a textual montage of all the crazy things I've written, or researched, or done, though it may be germane to point out that if you happen to be a literary agent, I have also written a novel about it. Anyway, all this is to say that I think I know a little bit about writing, and over the nearly five and a half years since I've done this job, I've learned a great deal about a lot of things. But I'm not by any means a super-genius. What I think makes me successful in my job is a combination of a pathologically Protestant work ethic and having learned some strategies to write quickly, thoroughly, and effectively. The biggest skill I have is in "hacking" papers – as in, working smarter, not harder, and figuring out the best ways to fake until I make it. If I can write A+ papers on books I've never read or for courses I've never even attended, then what's stopping **you**? If I can fake it every time despite, in many cases, not knowing anything about the class, then I'm confident **you can, too**. There are weaknesses aplenty in the academic system, and you can use those to your advantage to write papers.

I know every possible argument someone could make about my job, and I'm not interested in arguing (that's for another book…see my business plan?). However, I think it's better for everyone if instead of paying me a fortune to write a paper, people just learn some tips from this book – and see if they can write themselves. Students will learn, morals will be upheld, and I'll maybe get a little bit more sleep. So, I developed this book over the course of a few caffeine-fueled weeks.

How This Book Works

How should you use this book? Well, if you have a deadline in just a couple hours, I hope you skip past the introduction. Go to the chapter corresponding to the issue that's giving you the most trouble, and check out the "Quick Tips" along the way, which are brief recaps of, obviously, some of my quickest tips. When you've hit your deadline and gotten some sleep, come back and read the book all the way through. If you're not facing down a deadline, start from the beginning and proceed apace.

The chapters are arranged following a pretty logical progression through the writing process: Research, Actual Writing, Structure, and Formatting, though as you'll see, I will encourage you to think of these processes as interrelated, rather than as concrete steps. Just like with my work, I hope to make it clear to you that this is a judgment-free environment. You have a task, you're having trouble, and I'm here to help you have less trouble with it.

In this book, I'll also work you through some of my own research processes. Even if you're writing something very different, I hope that seeing the process applied to a real project clarifies how you can do it. I have a lot of degrees, but at the end of the day I'm just a regular person. If I can write papers without doing the reading, then so can you.

As I said above, there are many intractable, ingrained problems in academia. Some are recent, some have always existed, and some are just emerging. Some of the results of these problems are that people desperately need a credential, that professors may mean well but not have the economic incentive to teach as they would like, and that those who simply want a credential may end up in classes that they truly despise. I can't change the systemic pressures that push students towards outsourcing papers and using services like mine, but I *can* offer them a resource that empowers them to be less likely to use this method.

So, let's get started!

CHAPTER 1

Research: Work Smarter, Not Harder

et's face it. Research is tedious, and if you don't care about the subject, it can feel downright excruciating. It's probably even harder if you haven't exactly been keeping up with the course. In other words, even motivated students may find that they can skate by without doing the reading. That's OK. My top research tips follow. They assume that you're writing a paper that requires a certain number of sources beyond assigned class readings (the dreaded source scavenger hunt). However, even if you're not, my first tips will help.

Quick Tip:

There are many free programs that will generate perfectly-formatted citations and bibliography pages for you. Some great options: Mendeley (https://www.mendeley.com), EndNote (www.EndNote.com) , and Zotero, an open-source option (www.Zotero.org) .

I've mostly only used Mendeley. Which programs have you used? Are there any I'm missing? Get in touch on Twitter: @IamDeleuzienne #WorkSmarterNotHarder

Citation Management Software: Your new best friend

If I could give you *just one weird trick that professors hate*, this would be it. Your uptight English 101 teacher will shrilly assume this is not the case, but a powerful program like Mendeley – my personal favorite – generates perfect citations and bibliographies by coordinating with MS Word. It even has a plugin for your browser that will let you cite webpages and other materials. EndNote and Zotero are other options, but since I've hardly used them I won't talk about them much.

Mendeley has some features you might like, especially if you haven't done the reading. For example, "Mendeley search" lets you search the entire Mendeley catalog for sources on a term you enter. For another, Mendeley is owned by a major academic publishing company, so if you drop PDF's published by Elsevier into it, the software probably already "knows" the metadata (the title, author, year, journal, etc.), which will save you a couple minutes. You can install virtually any citation style, too.

The first time I used Mendeley, I had a nerdier moment than the first time I used a smartphone. I just downloaded a PDF and dropped the file into the program, and it extracted the publication data. Then, I searched for the source I wanted to use in my Word document. It generated a perfectly-formatted citation and created a bibliography that changed if I decided to switch to a different citation style (more on this later). Where was this the whole time I was doing my PhD? I swear, professors have some kind of cabal to try and keep this program a secret. As far as I can tell, it's mostly due to ignorance and a refusal to believe that it really works. That's stupid and the doubters are wrong. Just use it.

EasyBib.com is another site that provides a similar service, albeit one splattered with ads. It's also not free. *Moreover*, it is not as good as a dedicated software program, but if you have an older computer that can't handle Mendeley, or if you are using a cheap-o word processor (again...don't), or stuck somewhere without your own computer, it can be a good option, though I personally think it is crazy to pay for an inferior service when superior programs are free. I find this service is best for shorter, humanities-based papers with only a couple of sources, like the ones you write for English class on a specific book.

EndNote is another software option you can try, though I've never used it. Back when I was in my PhD, my university library canceled three training sessions in a row, so I gave up on trying to learn EndNote. From what I understand, this software is not free, but some colleges and universities may offer subscriptions to their students.

Microsoft Office has some increasingly good built-in features, but they are probably the weakest option here. They might be good if you have a quick paper with just a couple of sources, but I'd recommend it as a last option. However, software changes rapidly and just in the years I've been writing, Office's citation and bibliography features have improved rapidly.

Whichever option you use, it's going to be a powerful tool that will help you with this assignment and perhaps the rest of your education.

Now you've installed your citation management program. Fantastic. But you still have to find some content to cite, so let's move on.

But if you're still not convinced, pause for a moment and gaze in wonder at this chart. Do you spend too much time doing things on the left-hand side?

Before citation management software	After
Manually tabbing bibliography entries for the hanging indent	Automatically formatted bibliography
Looking up each source's metadata (author, DOI, etc.)	Database that has most sources and user-friendly interface for adding new ones
Excruciating process to manually update citations	Automatically updated, often with Word plug-in
Hard to keep sources centralized	Keep sources in one location
Spend years on Purdue OWL looking up arcane citation conventions	Computer does it.
Hours updating citations & bibliography to change citation style (e.g., MLA to Chicago)	Click and be amazed!

Consider this:

If you don't have to worry about the hairsplitting, excruciating details of overly fussy citation styles, then you can just focus on producing your essay.

That's magical! Freeing! Empowering!

Do you have other tips or apps you'd recommend? Get in touch on Twitter: @IamDeleuzienne

Using the Best Online Tools to Fake It

So now you're on the hunt for some sources. Be ready to take notes. I like to do this in the document I will ultimately write the paper in, and I recommend you do this (Plus, you can prime it with the pre-formatted citations when you use your citation manager). Be ready to glean some quick quotes as you read. This is about more than just getting quotes. It's about the psychological game, too. **The first sentence / paragraph / page is always the hardest, so make it easier on yourself by getting some content to use right away.** When you're no longer staring down a completely blank page, it gets a lot easier to get moving and to keep that momentum going.

Google Scholar

Google Scholar is a great tool not just because it lets you search for relevant terms, but also because you can search in a granular (i.e., highly specific) way. Did your professor say to only use articles written in the past 5 years? Great, check that box off in Google Scholar. Now, of course, you will likely have to deal with the garbage of academic publishing and go through a veritable obstacle course to download the files through your university's library (especially if you are off-campus). Make it easier on yourself. Look for sources with a PDF linked, as in the below screen cap.

I'm hungry, so let's research "food deserts" (This is also a great topic for social science classes. You're welcome!).

Google

"food deserts"

Scholar

About 8,610 results (0.07 sec)

My Citations

Articles

Case law

My library

Any time
Since 2017
Since 2016
Since 2013
Custom range...

2012 — 2017

Search

Sort by relevance
Sort by date

✓ include patents
✓ include citations

✉ Create alert

How to identify food deserts: measuring physical and economic access to supermarkets in King County, Washington
J Jiao, AV Moudon, J Ulmer... - ... journal of public ..., 2012 - ajph.aphapublications.org
Objectives. We explored new ways to identify **food deserts**. Methods. We estimated physical and economic access to supermarkets for 5 low-income groups in Seattle–King County, Washington. We used geographic information system data to measure physical access:
Cited by 90   Related articles   All 13 versions   Cite   Save

[HTML] nih.gov

[BOOK] Characteristics and influential factors of **food deserts**
P Dutko, M Ver Ploeg, TL Farrigan - 2012 - ers.usda.gov
Abstract USDA's Economic Research Service previously identified more than 6,500 food desert tracts in the United States based on 2000 Census and 2006 data on locations of supermarkets, supercenters, and large grocery stores. In this report, we examine the
Cited by 86   Related articles   All 2 versions   Cite   Save   More

[PDF] usda.gov

Distance to store, food prices, and obesity in urban **food deserts**
B Ghosh-Dastidar, D Cohen, G Hunter, SN Zenk... - American journal of ..., 2014 - Elsevier
Background Lack of access to healthy foods may explain why residents of low-income neighborhoods and African Americans in the US have high rates of obesity. The findings on where people shop and how that may influence health are mixed. However, multiple policy
Cited by 66   Related articles   All 13 versions   Cite   Save

[HTML] nih.gov

Food deserts: Governing obesity in the neoliberal city
J Shannon - Progress in Human Geography, 2014 - journals.sagepub.com
Studies of '**food deserts**', neighborhoods in which healthy food is expensive and/or difficult to find, have received much recent political attention. These studies reflect the popularity of a social ecology in public health, rising concerns over an obesity 'epidemic', and the
Cited by 63   Related articles   All 10 versions   Cite   Save

[PDF] uga.edu

Reestablishing healthy food retail: changing the landscape of **food deserts**
A Karpyn, C Young, S Weiss - Childhood Obesity (Formerly ..., 2012 - online.liebertpub.com
Conclusion While it is clear that a variety of approaches are underway, what is less clear is which approaches will be most effective. Research dollars instrumental for understanding impacts and teasing out effects are limited. Furthermore, initiatives such as the economic
Cited by 40   Related articles   All 7 versions   Cite   Save

[PDF] researchgate.ne

Look at that – a whole bunch of great sources with PDF's linked (note that links expire, and some of these, especially ones on Research Gate or Academia.edu, tend to disappear often). Also note that if you have access to a university library, it's a lot easier to get these sources. However, if you are not on campus, or if you do not have access to library resources off-campus or if you have no idea how to use your library's online portal, this is a good approach to finding sources.

Another important tool from Google Scholar is the "Cite" button, now represented by a graphical icon that looks like quotation marks (it changed during the time I was writing this book). Use this with caution, since a lot of data in Google Scholar is incorrect or incomplete. If the source has been entered correctly, however, this will help you copy/paste a perfectly formatted citation.

Google Books

Google Books is another important tool. Even if you haven't done the readings, most books are on here and you can search for key words that might appear in the book. This will help you avoid the telling mistake of only quoting from the introduction or worse, the back cover. Sometimes this "front-loaded" quote might be all you can find, however. In my experience, far too many professors are bean counters looking for little more than that you have hit the mandated number of sources and quotes. So, if the alternative is no quotes at all because you have not read and do not have a copy of the book, just use a bunch of quotes from one section in the book. Remember: A completed and handed-in paper, however imperfect, is better than no paper.

Keep in mind that you might have to think creatively here. If the first word you are looking for doesn't appear, look for synonyms. Are you working on a paper about gender, and searching for "feminism?" Try "women," "masculinity," "gender," "sex roles," and so on. You get the idea. Also keep in mind older books tend to use older terms.

Kindle

Another tool I like to use is the Kindle app on my computer. The device is great, but you'll want it on your computer for ease of copying and pasting quotes. I love my Kindle for regular reading, and one feature that is particularly useful is seeing how many other people have highlighted a passage in a book. You can look at a book's most highlighted or popular passages, which is a great way to add those mandated secondary sources without actually reading or understanding them. It might be that I have an old Kindle and only use it for "fun" reading (yes, that's a thing), but the software offers better study tools and makes it easier to look for specific words and phrases. When you copy text from Kindle (this is not available in all Kindle files, but you can do it in most of them) it even brings a citation with it.

Note that in many cases, Kindle files do not have page numbers. Now, a reasonable professor will look at your bibliography / works cited page and understand that you are working with a digital file, because they'll see "Kindle edition" on there. However, many professors seem to be unreasonable. In lieu of a page number for an unpaginated book, you can add the Kindle location number. I usually do this with a footnote explaining that the Kindle version of the book is unpaginated and that the numbers refer to location numbers in the file. You can also write "n.p.," but this might provoke your professor's ire.

Goodreads

I love Goodreads as a social network, because I'm a nerd, but also because it offers one great feature that will be relevant to you: "Favorite quotes." You haven't read *To Kill a Mockingbird*, you say? No problem. Google "Goodreads.com *To Kill a Mockingbird* quotes" (or whatever book you're looking for), or enter it into the search field on Goodreads.com itself. Then, look at the favorite quotes, which users have helpfully entered for you. Many are even tagged with themes and ideas or character names. Be careful because **these quotes seldom have page numbers**, and the ones that are there may correspond to a different edition of the book than the one you have (or that your professor expects you to have). If that's the case, a great strategy is to find the quote, then go to Google Books or whatever edition of the book you are using and find the page number. Paste the quotes back into your document and add the appropriate citation. Bam, now you have some quotes from the book that you can work with, without ever having actually cracked open the book (or double-clicked on the file).

Brilliant! And you know, *To Kill a Mockingbird* is highly overrated anyway. But that's a topic for another book...

Making Wikipedia Work Without Citing It

If you're starting from a topic you are totally unfamiliar with (not that this has ever happened to me ;-)), a good place to get oriented is Wikipedia. No, don't cite it. But despite how maligned it is by those who presumably despise free and open information, most entries require sources. I find that this is particularly useful for history papers. Don't quote Wikipedia, but **do** go there to get a good overview of a subject – and to find some of the most important sources that are cited for this new-to-you subject. Use it as an air traffic controller that directs you to your next stop. Many Wikipedia articles have direct quotes from sources you could use anyway. Here's an example of a Wikipedia source list, from the Wikipedia article for "Porter's Five Forces Analysis" (a very common topic for undergraduate business courses).

References [edit]

1. ^ Michael E. Porter, "How Competitive Forces Shape Strategy," May 1979 (Vol. 59, No. 2), pp. 137-145.
2. ^ Michael Porter, Nicholas Argyres, & Anita M. McGahan, "An Interview with Michael Porter", *The Academy of Management Executive* 16:2:44 at JSTOR
3. ^ Michael Simkovic, *Competition and Crisis in Mortgage Securitization*
4. ^ Tang, David (21 October 2014). "Introduction to Strategy Development and Strategy Execution". Flevy. Retrieved 2 November 2014.
5. ^ Kevin P. Coyne & Somu Subramaniam, "Bringing Discipline to Strategy, *The McKinsey Quarterly*, 1996, (Vol. 33, No. 4), pp. 14-25.
6. ^ Brandenburger, A. M., & Nalebuff, B. J. (1995). The Right Game: Use Game Theory to Shape Strategy. Harvard Business Review, (Vol. 73, No. 4), 57-71. PDF
7. ^ Michael E. Porter. "The Five Competitive Forces that Shape Strategy", Harvard Business Review, January 2008 (Vol. 88, No. 1), pp. 78-93. PDF
8. ^ Wernerfelt, B. (1984), A Resource-based View of the Firm, Strategic Management Journal, Vol. 5: pp. 171-180 PDF

Further reading [edit]

• Coyne, K.P. and Sujit Balakrishnan (1996),*Bringing discipline to strategy, The McKinsey Quarterly*, No.4.
• Porter, M.E. (March–April 1979) *How Competitive Forces Shape Strategy, Harvard Business Review*.
• Porter, M.E. (1980) *Competitive Strategy*, Free Press, New York.
• Porter, M.E. (January 2008) *The Five Competitive Forces That Shape Strategy, Harvard Business Review*.
• Ireland, R. D., Hoskisson, R., & Hitt, M. (2008). *Understanding business strategy: Concepts and cases.* Cengage Learning.
• Rainer R.K. and Turban E. (2009), *Introduction to Information Systems* (2nd edition), Wiley, pp 36–41.
• Kotler P. (1997), *Marketing Management*, Prentice-Hall, Inc.
• Mintzberg, H., Ahlstrand, B. and Lampel J. (1998) *Strategy Safari*, Simon & Schuster.

Look at all those sources! Sources for miles (or kilometers if that's your thing!)! Now, even if you are not a particular expert in this particular topic, you can look like one in your paper. Obviously, getting other sources is ideal, and you'll have to cross-check these to make sure they are valid. However, it's way better than having *zero* sources.

Bonus tip:

If the topic is <u>really</u> *technical or you* <u>really</u> *don't get it, or if English is not your first language, try Simple English Wikipedia, or a google search for "[topic] kids," or "[topic]+ ELI5" (Reddit-speak for "Explain Like I'm 5"). Sometimes kids' sites aren't just for kids.*

Do you have other tips or apps you'd recommend? Get in touch on Twitter: @IamDeleuzienne

Other Web Sources

There's so much out there that evaluating what is quality can be hard. Try to avoid sources that are just "content farms" (sites that create content solely to rank highly in search results, but that offer little new content). Avoid ad-splattered sites that repeat the search terms over and over (they are optimized for search engines and ad revenue). There are lots of good sources on relatively old (say, prior to 2010) .edu sites. This is because in the past, more professors were willing to create course content on public sites, instead of the third-party, for-profit classroom management sites that often partner with corporations and hence, shut this information off to the world. Lots of courses have online syllabi, information, and even lecture notes, so if your professor's information is confusing, you might find information from a professor who's clearer or more your style. As a bonus, these syllabi might offer potential sources to use for the paper. However, you may have to dig around to find author and date information so you can accurately cite them. The site that usually pops up from the search might have the information you need, but you might have to navigate back to the "home" page to find the author, year, etc.

With the strategies I have given you, you will easily find high-quality journal articles and books, so you have no need to look for garbage online sources. However, some topics are too recent or fresh for the glacial pace of academic publishing, so you will want to make sure you choose high-quality sources. Look for sites with **a clear author name, date of publication,** and **relatively few ads** (they are annoying, and can also be red flags for content farms). Some good sources for high-quality "hot takes" or essays can be Huffington Post, a professor's professional blog (hosted on their official webpage or on their own professional page), the <u>Stanford Encyclopedia of Philosophy</u> (HIGHLY recommended!), Medium.com, and, with a few caveats, About.com. Only use About.com articles if the author is clearly listed and an expert (check their biography). Some authors on this site are actual PhD's, but others are writing from their own "life experience."

Reading and Synthesizing Without Really Doing Either

Now you've gathered your sources. Time to research – or "research." I know this may seem like this is the tough part. I know you're looking at this stack of sources and wondering, "How the *hell* am I going to read all this?" The good news is, **you don't have to**. For most journal articles, **you just need to read the abstract**. If you want to understand it better, read the introduction and conclusion. Most journals are organized with these subheadings, although in the humanities sometimes they are not. Make friends with the abstract. You can think of this as a super-concentrated version of the paper. Add water (or bullshit) and stir. I'm not saying this is how academia works, but...

Hmm, time to end this chapter before I get in trouble.

Quick Tip:

If you are truly pressed for time, or if you cannot access a journal article, **just read the abstract**. Then if you have time to read the rest, focus on the **discussion, methodology,** and introduction. Also, look at the bibliography for additional sources you could cite.

What parts of a journal article do you find the most useful? Get in touch on Twitter: @IamDeleuzienne

Regardless, if you don't intend to read the whole thing – and I encourage you **not** to – read smart, meaning from the top down. Don't start at the beginning and read to the end, especially with journal articles. Instead, try this very rough map, understanding that many works will deviate from these exact headings:

1. Abstract
   a. From the abstract alone, you have an elevator pitch version of the work. This part of the paper, is required in APA and in most academic journals, offers a brief, highly concentrated summary. The quality and length can vary, and sometimes it's just unpaid interns who write these, rather than the authors. Overall, it offers a snapshot of the hypothesis, methods, results, and even the findings. If you're in a pinch and don't have time to read, or can't get the article in time thanks to the evils of academic publishing, this is a great way to get the "Cliffs Notes" version of the study.
2. Conclusion
   a. Although some simply offer a brief reiteration of the abstract, many will also succinctly state what it is that the study or article accomplished.
3. Methodology
   a. Here, you can get information about how the study was done. This can help you generate content for your paper, especially if the methods are subject to criticism. **For example: You can always milk a sentence or two out of studies deploying methods using self-reported information such as surveys and very small sample sizes (i.e., studies with very few participants).**
4. Discussion
   a. This is usually where the authors discuss the implications of their work. The "bigger picture" conclusions are usually here.
5. Introduction
   a. Often repeats much of the same information as the abstract, but also sets out the hypothesis and thesis of the study.
6. Literature review
   a. This is a great place to get the gist of the academic conversation, as the authors will typically describe previous studies, their theoretical framework, and otherwise sum up what others have said.

Then, once you read, **read in a "funnel."** Read the first paragraph of each section, and read the first (**topic**) sentence for each paragraph. **Skim** for words like conclusion, findings, and so on. Because it's always important to be able to criticize research, and because criticizing research takes up space in the paper, **pay attention to the methodology** if you have the luxury of time to do so.

Applying it

Oh no…turns out tomorrow your English 201 professor wants you to hand in a five-page paper on Jane Austen's *Mansfield Park*. The instructions are vague: "Write at least five pages on a theme you've identified in the novel. Use at least 3 secondary sources and 6 passages from the book. Standard formatting: 1-inch margins, 12 point Times New Roman font." You have not read this book. You have never opened this book. You may not have ever even heard of this book. You are not sure this is even a real book. The theme you have already identified is anxiety, but it might not be in the book. You can panic, drop the class, take an F, grovel for an extension that you know you won't get….or you can **research smarter**. Let's try my methods. The first thing we *won't* do is reach for the book and try to read it, just in case you were wondering.

First, let's mine some quotes for *Mansfield Park*. Add the book to Mendeley or whatever citation management program you are using. Next, check out Wikipedia. Does this book have a summary on Wikipedia? Yes, it does. Sweet: A nice plot summary awaits you! Next, check out the book on Goodreads.com and look at the popular quotes. Grab a couple and put them into your document, as below: We'll find page numbers in a bit. Look at the tags. Note that most of the quotes in this particular example focus on "fan" service, in that they reflect romance, characters, and so on. That is not usually a great topic for this kind of paper. If this means you do not find quotes that connect to the themes you want, then you can try Googling "important quotes," but keep in mind this will bring you to ad-splattered sites that provide pretty shallow analysis. At the same time, sometimes you just need the quotes. After a few minutes poring through Goodreads, this is what I have on my document, the one that will become a paper. I began to sense a theme about women and thinking or education:

DUE TOMORROW: <u>5 page</u> paper on Mansfield park
5 pages, 3 sources, 6 quotes

""Good-humoured, unaffected girls, will not do for a man who has been used to sensible women. They are two distinct orders of being." (Austen)

""There is nothing like employment, active indispensable employment, for relieving sorrow. Employment, even melancholy, may dispel melancholy." (Austen)

"She was not often invited to join in the conversation of the others, nor did she desire it. Her own thoughts and reflections were habitually her best companions." (Austen)

""... But he recommended the books which charmed her leisure hours, he encouraged her taste, and corrected her judgment; he made reading useful by talking to her of what she read, and heightened its attraction by judicious praise." (Austen)

""She began to feel that she had not yet gone through all the changes of opinion and sentiment, which the progress of time and variation of circumstances occasion in this world of changes." (Austen)

""If any one faculty of our nature may be called *more* wonderful than the rest, I do think it is memory. There seems something more speakingly incomprehensible in the powers, the failures, the inequalities of memory, than in any other of our intelligences. The memory is sometimes so retentive, so serviceable, so obedient - at others, so bewildered and so weak - and at others again, so tyrannic, so beyond control! - We are to be sure a miracle every way - but our powers of recollecting and of forgetting, do seem peculiarly past finding out." (Austen)

Have I ever read this book for the purposes of the paper? Nope. Have I done more than skim the plot summary on Wikipedia? Nope. But now I have six quotes on a related theme, and a basic understanding of the plot. Time to get the secondary sources. For this example, let's ignore the sources that are linked in Wikipedia and concentrate on using Google Scholar.

"mansfield park" gender

About 4,740 results (0.11 sec)

Mansfield Park: Slavery, Colonialism, and Gender
M Ferguson - Oxford Literary Review, 1991 - euppublishing.com
Mansfield Park (1814) is a eurocentric, post-abolition narrative that intertwines with a critique
of **gender** relations and posits a world of humanitarian interactions between slave-owners
and slaves. As such, following the successful passage of the Abolition Bill in 1807, **Mansfield**
☆ 𝟿𝟿 Cited by 61 Related articles All 3 versions

[BOOK] **Mansfield park**
[PDF] jausten.it
J Austen - 1980 - books.google.com
... During this time, Austen published four of her major novels: Sense and Sensibility (181 I); Pride
and Prejudice (I813); **Mansfield Park** (1814); and Emma (1816 ... VIVIEN JONES is Professor of
Eighteenth-Century **Gender** and Culture in the School of English, University of Leeds. ...
☆ 𝟿𝟿 Cited by 795 Related articles All 214 versions 𝄞

Jane Austen and Edward Said: gender, culture, and imperialism
[PDF] georgetown.edu
S Fraiman - Critical Inquiry, 1995 - journals.uchicago.edu
... Totowa, NJ, 1983), pp. 11S19;Johnson,Jane Austen, pp. 106-8; and Moira Ferguson, "**Mansfield Park**: Slavery, Colonialism, and **Gender**," Oxford Literary Rezxiew
13, nos. 1-2 (1991): 118-39. On Bronte's ambiguous use of ...
☆ 𝟿𝟿 Cited by 117 Related articles All 7 versions

[CITATION] Regulating Readers: **Gender** and Literary Criticism in the Eighteenth-
Century Novel
E Gardiner - 1999 - Kendall Hunt
☆ 𝟿𝟿 Cited by 27 Related articles 𝄞

[CITATION] Jane Austen and discourses of feminism
D Looser - 1995 - philpapers.org
... Mind; Philosophy of Religion; M&E, Misc. Value Theory: Value Theory; Aesthetics;
Applied Ethics; Meta-Ethics; Normative Ethics; Philosophy of **Gender**, Race, and
Sexuality; Philosophy of Law; Social and Political Philosophy; Value ...
☆ 𝟿𝟿 Cited by 61 Related articles 𝄞

[CITATION] 'That Abominable Traffic': **Mansfield Park** and the Dynamics of Slavery
J Lew - History, Gender, and Eighteenth-Century Literature, 1994
☆ 𝟿𝟿 Cited by 32 Related articles

[BOOK] The Postcolonial Jane Austen
Y Park, RS Rajan - 2015 - books.google.com
This volume offers a unique contribution to both postcolonial studies and Austen scholarship
by:" examining the texts to illumine nineteenth century attitudes to colonialism and the
expanding Empire" revealing a new range of interpretations of Austen's work, each shaped
☆ 𝟿𝟿 Cited by 52 Related articles All 2 versions 𝄞

The Politics of Silence:" **Mansfield Park**" and the Amelioration of Slavery
[PDF] academia.edu
GE Boulukos - Novel: A forum on fiction, 2006 - JSTOR
Page 1. The Politics of Silence: **Mansfield Park** ... The first section of this essay considers Said's
methods in inter- preting **Mansfield Park**, including his commitment to an ideal of interpretation
as breaking the silences of the past, dependent on the model of "the colonial ...
☆ 𝟿𝟿 Cited by 34 Related articles All 5 versions

[CITATION] Decolonising **Mansfield Park**
J Wiltshire - Essays in Criticism, 2003 - academic.oup.com
... Hence in Moira Ferguson's influential 1991 article '**Mansfield Park**, Slavery,
Colonialism and **Gender**' there is no question of **Mansfield Park** being idealised,
as in Said's piece: instead it is a mirror image of the slave estate. 'The ...
☆ 𝟿𝟿 Cited by 26 Related articles All 3 versions

Sources for days! For my paper, I'm going to focus on the Ferguson 1991 source, the 2015 Park / Rajan book, and the Fraiman (1995) source. These have links to places where I can download the journal articles (for Ferguson and Fraiman) or preview the book (good for Park / Rajan). My next steps would be to import the PDF's into Mendeley and then, if possible, search the journal articles for words and phrases. Note that not all PDF's are searchable, and there are often errors, so always double-check any text you might paste. Just by searching for feminism, I found some good passages in the Fraiman source:

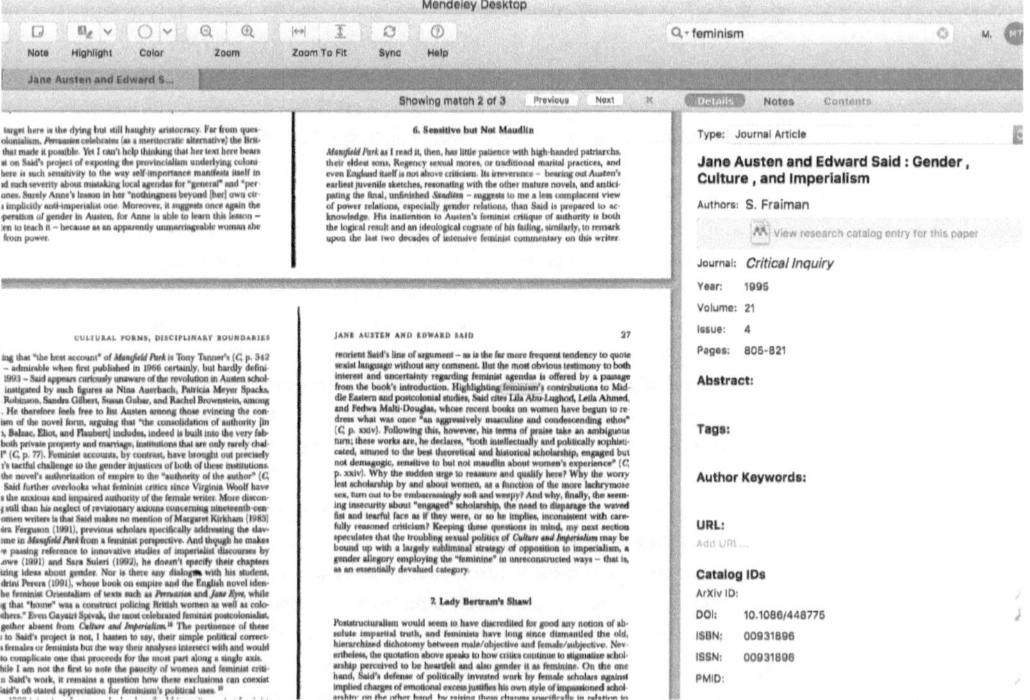

As you can see, we're doing the same thing with the secondary sources that we did with the primary sources. Moreover, as we compile more sources into the document, *it is filling up with words*. We only had a blank page just a few minutes ago, and no clue what this book was even about, but now we have quotes on a theme and the secondary literature to back it up. It might not be the most brilliant paper on earth, but it's sure better than nothing. It's progress. Score. *You can do this.*

Quick tip:

*Can't find the city where a book was published? Just write "New York." All of the "big five" publishers are located in New York City. The majority of academic publishers can be found by Googling the university. If the book is non-academic, e.g., a novel, and you **really** can't find the place of publication, just put "New York" as a last resort. Trust me, nobody will ever check.*

A Pairing Menu for Great Source Websites

Here are some sites I use frequently, in no particular order, and what types of assignments or courses they "pair" well with. Just pretend they are wines or beers as you peruse this menu:

Stanford Encyclopedia of Philosophy — Written by professors, peer-reviewed, and designed for students (though sometimes seems aimed at upper-level students). A great way to learn about theory and philosophy, or at least fake your way through. **Pairs well with: Philosophy, political science, history, literature, ethics, sociology.**

Arts and Letters Daily — A smorgasbord of great information updated daily. A great way to find high-quality sources for humanities classes, or just to exercise your brain. **Pairs well with: Composition, English / literature, philosophy, personal development.**

KidsHealth.org: An easy-to-read site that explains science and health. Great if you're totally lost in a science or health class, or just trying to Dr. Google yourself. I have found more useful information there outlining, say, how the digestive system works than I have in actual college textbooks. You might not want to actually cite it, but if you are not picking up on something, it has great explanations. **Pairs well with: Nursing, anatomy, health, all the various "flavors" of science.**

EasyBib.com — I recommend this site with a big caveat. If you're in a pinch and can't work with Mendeley (which will also generate copy-friendly citations on the web, by the way), and need MLA citations only — then EasyBib.com can help. Especially good if you're rushing to complete an English paper. **Pairs well with: Frantically making an MLA-style Works Cited in the library just before class. That's basically it. It's like the Milwaukee's Best of websites. You can do better but sometimes you just can't be bothered, and if you choose it, I'm going to judge you a little because there are just so many better things out there.**

NYTimes.com — The paper of record continues to NOT FAIL as you can search news archives going back to 1851 and access high-quality reporting and opinion writing reflecting a wide variety of perspectives. You can read something like 10 articles free a month without a subscription, and in many cases, you can likely access it through your school's library portal. There are also discounts for student subscriptions. **Pairs well with: History, current events, politics, composition, sociology, pop culture, literature (e.g., book reviews), science (for news of major discoveries).**

RogerEbert.com — Although Roger Ebert passed away in 2013, virtually all of the reviews he ever wrote are archived here. New content is also added daily. There may be no better way to begin to write a film appreciation paper (especially if you haven't seen the movie) than starting with Ebert's take on the film. Ebert was a great writer and also touched upon cultural and social issues, too, so this site could help with history or sociology papers as well (e.g., look up reviews of documentaries about social issues). **Pairs well with: Film, obviously; history and sometimes sociology.**

GradeSaver.com — This is another site I recommend with some big reservations. Keep in mind that they are making money from clicks and traffic, so they have little incentive to provide high-quality content. However, they do have a very diverse array of study guides for almost every novel you're likely to be assigned. These are **not** vetted for quality, so proceed with caution. They say the essays are written by Harvard students, but I believe that is a suspect claim. **Pairs well with: English, Education (you know, those "Kiddie / YA Lit" classes), just getting a quick summary to fake having read it.**

MetMuseum.org — The online home of the Metropolitan Museum of Art in New York City, the online collection is just as vast and impressive. Many thousands of items in the Museum's collection are beautifully photographed online and *paired with expertly-written essays that will explain the significance of the piece*. There is also a beautiful timeline of art history on their site. **Pairs well with: Art appreciation / history / theory, history, classics / mythology, politics, world cultures, and even anthropology as the timeline goes back to ca. 8000 BCE.**

Gutenberg.org — You spent your book money on beer, huh? You can't find your copy of *Oliver Twist*? Lucky for you, Gutenberg.org has been digitizing most out-of-copyright (read: Old) works for decades now. **Pairs well with: English classes dealing with books written before 1925, history (especially eighteenth and nineteenth century)**

CHAPTER 2

Actually Writing

Want one more way to put off the actual writing? Here's another tip. **Use Autocorrect.** Don't just use it for typos, though my rule is always "if I make a typo once, I'll probably make it again." *Also* use Autocorrect for acronyms and shortcuts to replace common words and phrases. Put your text speak into it and type like you do to your friends. I like to think of Autocorrect as part of a "Tinker-Toy" approach to writing, in which things are more modular and manufactured. Instead of building with words, you're building with phrases.

A few suggestions and choices from my own list are in the table below; as you can tell, I did not feel like scrolling much past "I" in the list:

You Type	You Get
AWA	As well as
Iot	in order to
ito	In terms of
Infosec	Information security
otoh	On the other hand,
isc	Information security compliance

For me, the key is less to identify a very specific phrase or sentence than it is to find out which commonly occurring phrases can be "hacked," saving me lots of time in the long run. However, your mileage may vary. The idea is to save time overall. **If you consistently make a typo in a word, as I just did (on purpose!) in this very sentence with the word "conssistently", run a spell check and set the corrector to auto-correct.** You probably already do this for misspellings, but work smarter: Use it to save time. If you're a slow typist and staring down a deadline in just a couple of hours, the five minutes that you save over the course of those hours can mean the difference between, say, running a final spellcheck, catching an error, or adding an elegant conclusion and not being able to do so.

QUICK TIP:

If you're a power-writer, and often find yourself writing the same paragraphs (or emails, etc.), try using a program like TextExpander to auto-expand snippets or abbreviations. This tool is great for the rest of your life, like if you are an officer in a club or send the same email to your roommates every day asking them to clean their dishes. ☺ As I always say, work smarter, not harder!

How do you work smarter, not harder? Get in touch on Twitter: @IamDeleuzienne

Psych yourself into writing

The first word of the first sentence of the first paragraph of the first page is often the hardest. Fight that by *just writing*. Don't second-guess yourself. **Just write**. I recommend setting a timer for 15 to 20 minutes. During that time, maximize the word processor window (note: This might interfere with the citation management program, but ideally, you've already gotten some quotes from there). **Write**. Do not let yourself press the backspace (temporarily cover it with paper or tape if you must!). Just write and don't even read it. **The psychological boost that you'll get from having your ideas *somewhere* is much more important than knowing you've written something perfect**.

I personally like the Pomodoro method, in which you work for 15 or 20 minutes, take a quick break, and then do another 15-to-20-minute set, with a longer break after 5 or 6 sets. However, some people tell me they find this difficult for getting into a flow. Either way, if you are having trouble, set a timer for a few minutes, eliminate all distractions, and just write a sentence. Then another. And another. Ultimately, this is how writing happens: Words become sentences, paragraphs, pages, and chapters.

After 20 minutes, if you are truly stuck, let yourself run a spell check. Don't edit, just fix the typos (and see if you can add any autocorrects). If you let yourself run a spell check occasionally when you're stuck, you'll use your time productively while also reducing the risk of missing embarrassing typos (If you find any in this book, let me know! I will revise and thank you in a future edition!).

The "Text Pasture:" Where old paragraphs go to retire

In my opinion, one of the worst feelings is having to work on something on a deadline when your mind wants to go elsewhere. The second-worst feeling, of course, is having written something good and having to cut it. One tool I like to use is what an old friend of mine called the "text pasture." What is this? It's a blank document you keep open as you write. If you cut something you like, you put it in the text pasture – you know, so it can romp and play in the fields with all the old dogs that got sent to the farm. Why do this? You'll feel less bad about cutting it, and you could probably use the cut text later for another paper. Plus, if your mind starts to wander (Spoiler: It will), this is a way to track those ideas your brain wants to run with while still getting stuff done.

Building out

Use your outline, if you have made one earlier. Outlines are great for getting started, although not everyone has the luxury of time to make one. But what if you haven't made an outline? Should you make one before you start writing, even if the professor isn't requiring it? What if you changed your topic? Instead of an outline, what I like to do is make what I'll call a textual outline. Remember how I said to read in a funnel? This strategy lets you *write* sort of like a funnel. Instead of a formal outline, just begin by writing the topic sentence for each paragraph.

The introduction and conclusion are usually freebies. Do them first. The introduction can set a template for the essay or paper. It's usually OK to write things like "First, this essay will discuss a historical overview of scholarship on *To Kill a Mockingbird*. Next, I turn to the contemporary academic conversation on this topic in order to show that this book may not endure for the next half century of its existence. Third, the essay explores different interpretations and some popular interpretations of the novel. Finally, I discuss the implications and avenues for future research." Note a few things I did there. First, I used some stilted, wordy phrases. Part of that is because most teachers have a knee-jerk gag reflex if you use the word "I," **even if professional academic journal articles would actually use it in an analogous** context. Second, I provided a snapshot – a kind of abstract for the whole paper. Third, I took up space. I call this meta-writing. Is it the best practice in the entire world? Does it lead to especially beautiful writing? No, but if you're choosing between meta-writing and *not* writing, or meta-writing and trying to find an excuse, guess which one is better? Plus, this is a skeleton. As you fill in the rest of the paper you can flesh out these sentences so they sound a bit less dry. Also, if you really want to pad it, you can use the future tense instead of the simple present to get a few more words in. Sure, it sounds like campaign promises, but "This essay will engage with the Humperdinck article in order to show…" sounds slightly more highfalutin, and more importantly, *contains more words*, than "This essay engages with the Humperdinck article in order to show…"

The conclusion, too, should just restate what you did (or planned to do) and offer some statements. It's OK to talk about topics that you didn't have space to cover, or things that there wasn't much information on. Returning to my example of *To Kill a Mockingbird*, you might write something like "Unfortunately, there are few Marxist interpretations of this novel. This is an avenue that scholars may wish to pursue."

At this point, if you've followed my approach, you will already have an introduction, a conclusion, and a topic sentence for each paragraph. What are some other tips? Gosh, I'm so glad you asked. Well, I asked myself. This is what too much writing does to you. Anyway, let's talk about making word and page counts.

Making word counts

If every single paper, ever, could be based on a word count, the world would be a much better and more rational place. If possible, ask your professor to give you a target word count for the assignment, rather than a vague page count. If they refuse, you know they are really old and still stuck in the days of cassette tapes and typewriters. This is because it's way too easy for students to tinker with margins, k e r n i n g , the fonts, and line spacing – and everyone knows it. For your reference, a double-spaced page, the kind that most professors want, is about 250-300 words in standard formatting and on standard U.S. letter page sizes (8.5 x 11" or 216 x 279 mm). I would say that more than 90% of the time, undergraduate professors want double-spacing. Outside the U.S., and particularly in Europe and Australia, A4 paper size (8.3" x 11.7" or 210 x 297 mm) is much more common. **In general, you should not really change the default formatting settings on your word processor**.

Making word count is about more than using the wordiest phrasings you can possibly imagine, and it involves more than padding with lots of big quotes. Those are both strategies you can use, but they will be blatantly obvious to any professor. Making word count can happen in many ways. The first, and most obvious, is to know what you're saying and have a lot to say. The second is to fluff out paragraphs. If you have said everything you want and you still aren't near the word count, ask yourself if you could add more transition sentences or "meta-writing." The third is to add a few more quote-unpack sections.

No……sleep……'til 'page count!

I personally like to write in single-space and then double-space it later. The psychological boost you get is incomparable when you put it into double-spacing and realize you've written twice as many pages. However, once you put it into double-spacing, the best thing you can do if you're trying to meet a page count is increase the number of lines. Imagine a paragraph.

A paragraph, like the one right above this paragraph right here. It'd be pretty easy to bulk that up, wouldn't it? Let's try it again, but let's add a couple words here and there to knock it onto the next line:

"I personally like to write in single-space and then double-space it later. The psychological boost you get is incomparable when you put it into double-spacing and realize you've written twice as many pages as it looks like you did. However, once you put it into double-spacing, the best thing you can do is increase the number of lines if you're trying to meet a page count. This is because each line takes up space, and fills up the pages, thus reducing the chance your professor will mark you down for writing too little. To illustrate: Imagine a paragraph."

See? I only added a few words, but milked a valuable line out of it. We're one line closer to the page count. Let's try it again but go to the *next* line!

"I personally like to write in single-space and then double-space it later. The psychological boost you get is incomparable when you put it into double-spacing and realize that you've written twice as many pages as it looks like you did. However, once you put it into double-spacing, the best thing you can do is increase the number of lines if you're trying to meet a specific minimum page count. This is because each line takes up space, and fills up the pages, thus reducing the chance your professor will mark you down for writing too little. Let's walk through an example together. Imagine a paragraph."

Note that I did not really add any new ideas in each iteration. I just added some more information and made it wordier. Again, this is not the world's greatest writing, and some professors will notice if you do this excessively. But realistically, few professors will really care if your writing style is excessively wordy. Nowadays, most grading is done with a rubric, which is a glorified checklist. Professors are encouraged to grade based on what an essay does, rather than what it doesn't do; when they do grade on what it doesn't do, it is usually based on objective criteria. In my experience, these objective criteria are usually based on citation formatting, more general document formatting, writing mistakes, the use of evidence, and the absence or presence of a thesis.

If you're just trying to fill in space, there are any number of formatting tricks you can use, though I do not recommend that you do things like change the font size or font, increase the margins (**Note**: On some laptops, like mine, MS Word sets the default margins to 1.25", presumably because it's easier to see on a small screen), jerry-rig the line spacing, or increase the kerning (a fancy term for the space between letters). These tricks will likely be obvious to your professor, so **use them at your own risk**.

QUICK TIP:

Have you ever come across an error in a quotation? Typos happen everywhere, and sometimes you have to quote things that are not in the Queen's English. Did you know you can use this to your word / space count advantage w*hile also asserting your impressive grammatical knowledge*? WOW! When you come across such errors, retain them in the quote and add [sic]. The term itself is Latin and is used to show a) that a quotation is exact and b) that the error was in the original.

Try this example from Incidents in the Life of a Slave Girl *by Harriet Jacobs:* "I ain't worth it,' said he" (Jacobs). You might be thinking: Wait, who puts "ain't" in a paper? But you can't change the quote, otherwise the Secret Plagiarism Committee will break your knees. So, what do you do?

"I ain't [sic] worth it,' said he" (Jacobs). Presto! Gain a word! If you want to go all in, the first time you quote from a work like this, write something like *"All grammatical errors have been retained to show the spirit / dialect of the original work"* in either the main text or as a footnote.

Do you have other word-bulking tips? *Let's have a conversation on Twitter: @IamDeleuzienne*

Bulking Up What You've Got When You've Hit the Wall

It's happened to all of us. It's 11 PM, the paper is due at 9:45 AM, and even though you absolutely, positively must hand in 5 double-spaced pages, you're on page 3 and don't have one more word about Russian serfs (or photosynthesis, or Charles Dickens, or a PESTLE analysis of Starbucks, or human resources management, or whatever) in you. At this point, you may be tempted to start playing with the margins, line spacing, or font. Don't do that except as an *absolute last resort.*

Try this instead. Take a break for a minute (do some push-ups, jumping jacks, something to get you moving and thinking). Maybe that will give you ideas. If not, go back to what you've written. Have you used any secondary sources? Is there a way to go back and add criticism of those sources, like by criticizing a methodology used in some of the sources you've used? For example, you could go back to where you mentioned a secondary resource and note that the author only focused on one author, that they ignored the author's other work, that they used a sample size of 2, etc.

Another way to bulk up paragraphs and sections is to **build transitions**. If possible, don't let the transitions be "meta-writing." Think about how one idea connects to the other. For example, for the *Mansfield Park* example, I might write "However, this quote simply shows that Fanny was enthralled by her cousin's book recommendations and was strongly formed by him. Does this mean that she has begun to fit in at Mansfield Park?" A question is an okay transition. Do it too much and it seems repetitive and forced, but it can be an effective bridge between ideas in the paper.

Reread your paragraphs and make sure each one has a topic sentence, content, and a transition to the next sentence. Often, especially if your deadline is soon, you are likely to find that you've forgotten a few of these. If not, just add more content, especially to smaller paragraphs. If you have nothing to say, make internal connections. Add phrases like "In contrast to the historical focus of [another author]" or "In contrast to the qualitative approach of [another author you've used]."

A great strategy, especially for a shorter paper, is a paragraph in which you define your terms. This could effectively take the place of the literature review in a longer paper, and if you've otherwise just jumped right into the content after the introduction paragraph, this can add content while ensuring that your argument is clearer. I don't mean to go run to the dictionary and offer definitions. Rather, you can write something like "For the purposes of this essay, the term *postmodern* springs from Baudrillard analysis…" or "The definition of *psychodynamic* used in this essay is based on Erikson's developmental framework…"

Get those sick word count gains, bro

Want to bulk up your writing like you do yourself at the gym? Ask yourself a few simple questions. Why say "like" when you can say "as well as"? This chart shows just a handful of my favorite swaps, for when you just *have* to add a couple of words to make a word count or try to squeeze your writing to the end of the page!

Why say…	When you can offer the following more verbose phrase? (These are just examples – feel free to tweak!)
Increase	Dramatically increase
Death	Tragic, untimely death
Describe	articulate
And	As well as
Their	His or her
Response	Meaningful response

Now	At this point in time

Modifying adverbs can be used, within reason, to bulk up word count as well. When "articulates" becomes, say, "truly articulates" you're one word closer. The same is true of adjectives. Phrases like "In a [year] journal article, [Author] argued…" are wordy, but can help work as both transitions as well as to increase word count. Prepositional phrases (e.g., "laws created in the modern era" instead of "modern laws") are also a subtler way to occasionally bulk up a sentence. **Many professors are wise to obvious word padding**, but with practice you can make it sound natural (to a degree), and if one or two sentences in your paper are the difference between hitting page count or not…a few wordy sentences won't be the worst offense committed in the name of academia. Look up your professor's publications if you don't believe me.

Charts, Tables, and Graphs

When is it appropriate to use charts, images, tables, and graphs? Unfortunately, their use is mostly restricted to the social and hard sciences, so you are a bit stuck if you're writing a paper on, say, German literature. I almost never use them, because at least at the undergraduate level, they are pretty obvious filler unless the paper is centered on data and processes. If you're tempted to include a chart or graph, you might be better served by "narrating" it and putting the process or data trend into your own words. Even if reading a sentence like this makes your eyes bleed, it still represents text on paper and that's what most rubric-wielding professors are into: "The rainfall in year 0 was 20 inches, and in year 1 it was 23. However, it declined slightly in year 2, to a low for the data set of 18 inches. Meanwhile, year 3 experienced the greatest rainfall at 27 inches." Wow, that was boring. I almost fell asleep just writing that. However, it was also words that fill up space on a page without defaulting to (more) obvious filler tactics. You don't have to be so in-depth, but if the alternative is writing nothing, or giving up, then this is an option to supplement other content and strategies.

Other tips

Here's a list, in no particular order, of some other strategies. Note that some are more applicable to certain types of papers than others.

1. If you are given the choice for a citation style, you can make the paper easier for yourself. If it's a word count paper, go for a parenthetical citation style, like APA or Harvard, since each citation will give you an extra few words. However, page counts are the easiest to hit when you use a footnote style like Chicago, since each citation will get you an extra line.
2. If you're hitting a **page count** goal and using **Chicago style**, make sure you are using a book's or journal's full title in the footnotes (at least in the initial mention). Academic titles are long and this could break it onto the next line. Similarly, you can use the long title in the first mention of the work in the main body. Given how pompous these titles are, that's a fluffing-up freebie that can often give you an extra line or more.
3. As I've said before, it is always useful to critique methods of studies in the social or natural sciences. Nitpicking is fun and it shows the professor you're thinking critically.
4. Meta-writing, in which you talk about writing, is another strategy. Use with caution, but this is especially useful for longer documents. Conclusions are little more than the amalgam of what you just said, so if you're stuck on the last paragraph, you're in luck. "This essay has shown [thesis]. Beginning with [first piece of evidence] and drawing upon [second piece of evidence] …" is a good structure.

5. I have mixed feelings about epigraphs, but they can be powerful in the humanities not just to introduce your paper and its argument (as I did in the front matter of this book), but to, you know, take up space. Overly long epigraphs, or multiple quotes used as them, can appear as obvious filler, however. If you haven't read the book, good sources for quotes are Goodreads and QuoteGarden.com (also check out that vintage website).

CHAPTER 3

Putting it all together: Argument & Structure

So, now you have both words *and* sources, and hopefully several pages of content. Congratulations on obtaining the building blocks of the paper! I told you that you could do it! Now you may wonder: How can you structure these parts to mold them into a paper? These days, professors usually offer a very tight script or "paint-by-numbers" prescription of what they want. I find these approaches to be horrible. They're the opposite of what the professor should be doing (Or, in many cases, the opposite of what he or she even *wants* to be doing, but that's for a different book). On the other hand, these approaches do you the favor of preventing you from having to think too deeply, especially about the structure of your argument.

However, if you don't have a very specific instruction sheet telling you what you should be saying and when, you might wonder how to structure your argument. Even if you have a "script" from your professor telling you how to structure the paper, you may be wondering how to achieve that or how to make it work. Therefore, I've divided this chapter into "macro" and "micro" structures: The macro structures deal with how to construct a paper and more global structures, while microstructures deal with smaller structures, such as paragraphs.

Macro

The five-paragraph essay is not necessarily the be-all and end-all of writing, but most academic writing follows this pattern or otherwise expands on it. An introduction, a few major points and observations, a conclusion emphasizing some directions of future research, and then you can get some sweet sleep. Right? It's not quite that simple. Although the general structure of introduction → main content → conclusion dominates most fields, here are some templates.

For a simple, English or humanities-based essay, here's one template or approach you could use:

I.   Introduction
    a.   Introduce central theme
    b.   Thesis
    c.   Overview of paper (If you didn't have time to make a formal outline, this is very helpful!)
II.   First passage or quote
    a.   Contextualize quote
    b.   Offer quote
    c.   Unpack and explain quote
    d.   Transition

III. Second passage or quote
   a. Contextualize quote
   b. Offer quote
   c. Unpack and explain quote
   d. Transition
IV. Third passage or quote
   a. Contextualize quote
   b. Offer quote
   c. Unpack and explain quote
   d. Transition
V. Conclusion
   a. Overview
   b. Discuss implications
   c. Questions that remain

For a social sciences approach, such as a problem-solution paper on a major issue, you might write something like this:

I. Introduction
   a. "Everything's going to hell in a handbasket" or, why this topic is a big problem
   b. Thesis including solution
   c. Overview of paper
II. Literature review
   a. Introduce first piece of evidence or first study
      i. Analyze, unpack
   b. Introduce second piece of evidence
      i. Analyze, Unpack
   c. Introduce third piece of evidence
      i. Analyze, unpack
III. Analysis
   a. Connection among studies / sources of evidence
   b. Theoretical framework: Why is this happening?
IV. Solution
   a. CHOOSE ONE: Political advocacy, suggestions for laws, suggestions for citizens
   b. What is preventing the solution?
V. Conclusion
   a. Discuss the implications. What does it mean that this is happening?
   b. Related topics that Future Researchers should investigate

Notice how these are fundamentally the same structure. For longer essays, you can go into more detail, offer more sources, offer a rebuttal, and so on, but the same Introduction → Content → Conclusion structure is still there. Even a dissertation generally follows the same rough format of Introduction → Existing literature → Case Studies → Conclusion (though the hard sciences do diverge from this format).

Micro

Now that you have a broad idea of how to structure your paper, it's time to sweat the small stuff. You are probably already familiar with the sandwich-type, topic sentence –> "meat" –> transition sentence paragraph structure, so I won't dwell too long on this subtopic. However, **just as you should read in a funnel, you should write in an hourglass**. Begin with a topic sentence, offer content, add a transition. I personally find this deadly dull and wish there was room for creativity and experimentation, especially because so much professional academic writing does not really use this structure (especially in the humanities). I'm not going to bean-count at you and claim that a paragraph must have X many sentences, though some professors insist on this. A good rule is 5 sentences or more. Here's an example of a boring paragraph that would probably be acceptable to most professors. This would fit in towards the end of the essay.

> "The issue of income inequality is a very serious one because it seems to defy the promise of the American Dream. If people are born into poverty and cannot escape it, then something is very wrong with society. [Source #1] showed how schools fail to prepare impoverished children for the demands of college education. [Source #2] showed how income inequality can have serious impacts on public health. Finally, [Source #3] explored the ways that the wealthy have concentrated their resources and smeared the mere idea of taxation and equality as "socialism." Can anything be done to save the American dream, or is our country doomed to oligarchy? Remarkably, there might still be hope."

Notice how this paragraph has a topic sentence, the requisite amount of content, and then a transition? It's like a sandwich. Except it's sort of like a boring, stale sandwich, and, most importantly, a sandwich in which the bread is stuck to the next sandwich: A chain of sandwiches. Delicious, but full of carbs. Carb-heavy – but helping your future, right?

CHAPTER **4**

Literally the Worst: Formatting

I know you've had it beaten into your head from the very beginning that you should submit a professional document. And it matters more than you might realize. Just as we have a subconscious bias for the people we have been acculturated to understand as attractive, so too are we drawn to neat, tidy documents and papers. It sucks. I hate it. The good news is that in the digital age, it is easier than ever to avoid careless mistakes and to turn in something that looks sharp. If you don't have to worry about printer ink, handwriting, crumbling up paper, and so on, then you're already in far better shape than past generations. Do as I say, not as I did for my entire life until everything went digital.

However, formatting can still look sloppy even in the digital age. If you've been following my recommendations, you should be able to avoid typos. However, even the best-spelled paper can still contain careless mistakes if you have grammatical mistakes or if formatting errors creep in, making margins, paragraphs, fonts, and so on look weird.

When seconds count, try editing during your breaks or when you're stuck. Everyone says to read your paper out loud. Nobody does that. Instead, try to read a paragraph, a page, or a sentence at a time.

Formatting Tips: Avoid Spelling and Grammar Mistakes

Make sure you've run 2 or 3 spellchecks per page. Not all in a row, but over the course of the project. Try doing it after you finish each paragraph. Read your paper over, at least briefly. Once you've been working on something for a long time, you reach a point of diminishing returns with respect to editing and being able to catch errors. This is why ideally you get the paper done six weeks ahead of time and have a professional editor or Oxford-educated tutor read it. But even motivated people don't live in the ideal. Make sure you're not misusing homonyms, like too, to, and two and they're, their, and there. Don't ever use an apostrophe in a plural, unless it's for an acronym or number: "Pizza's" is not OK (eating multiple pizzas is fine). "A lot" is actually two words (hey, you bump up your word count). "Whose" relates to possession and "who's" is a contraction. However, "1920's" **is** acceptable. Those kinds of careless errors are the worst. Don't blame me, blame the English language.

Formatting Tips: Comply with APA or Your Professor Will Probably Kill You

I loathe APA with the passion of 10,000 fiery suns. It's the Basic Bitch of citation styles, and I think it is a style that actually **infects** writing. I think that the long, mid-sentence citation breaks up your brain's ability to process information, and I think that for real APA hardliners and fundamentalists, the emphasis on bizarre, non-English capitalization does far more harm than good. Especially because of the uneven application of its more hairsplitting rules, you might have a professor one term who demands you write an abstract, and a professor another term who considers this filler. Easiest to just follow this soul-rending checklist.

Mandatory Soul-Rending Checklist for APA Compliance

1. Is my work in Times New Roman, size 12?
2. Are my margins 1" (2.54 cm)?
3. Is the first page UNNUMBERED?
   a. Go to Insert, Page Numbers, and align to the top of the page. UNCHECK "Number first page."

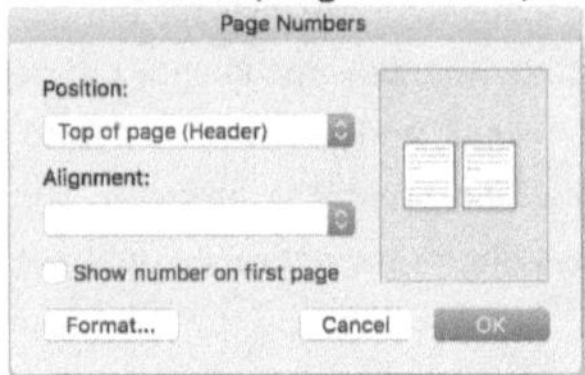

4. Are subsequent pages NUMBERED?
5. Does the first page say, "Running Head: SHORT TITLE OF PAPER IN CAPS" on the left?
   a. Double-click the top and type this. I have an autocorrect for "Rh," which might be worth doing if you write a lot of APA papers.
6. Do subsequent pages say "SHORT TITLE OF PAPER IN CAPS" on the left, with pages numbers on the right?
   a. Double-click and repeat.
7. Have I titled the final page "References" and centered "References" at the top of the page?
8. Did I generate an APA bibliography in Mendeley or another software program?
9. Did I make a title page that follows my professor's wishes and that includes my name, the date, the assignment and other information required? (I have seen this vary widely, so look up an APA title page template and tweak to your needs)
10. Are all internal citations in the format (Author, year) and (Author, year, p. X)?
11. Have I checked more exotic citation or formatting scenarios with Purdue OWL?
12. Am I dead on the inside?

Let me tell you, I couldn't despise APA more. Of all the formats that I've used and written in, including Bluebook (For legal writing), IEEE (for engineering), MHRA (for British people, apparently), and once some weird format used exclusively in a very specific journal about a very specific type of wildlife management in one very specific country, nothing was as picky. Frankly, I think that APA is often used as a power play. It's the hall monitor of citation styles. It's a way to mark down students for formatting at the expense of ignoring their voices and ideas, and that is despicable. Professors – and I know a few of you are reading this – you have *no idea* how many of my clients are people who are just utterly overwhelmed and frustrated by these formatting requirements. Of these, the vast, vast majority are being asked to write in APA. It really makes you think…

CHAPTER 5

Final Strategies and Useful Resources

I hope that this book has given you tips and strategies, but more importantly, confidence. You know more than you think you do. If you think of writing as just a way of talking, and of papers as putting your ideas into this format, it is a little more empowering. Ultimately, I wish education was better for everyone. I wish people had more creative assignments; I wish younger students learned writing in a positive and creative way; I wish people valued the written word, and I even wish your professors had better pay. Even though your professor may seem like a frustrating, inhuman, detail-obsessed wet blanket, they probably hate teaching and grading in this pedantic way just as much as you hate to do it, and they are probably making far less money than you might imagine. So, keep that in mind. Also, keep in mind that if you're stressed out and pulling an all-nighter about a paper now, there are things you can do to make it less unpleasant next time. This chapter will focus on offering you a compendium of resources to help you work smarter, not harder, on your future papers, even if it was too late for the one you just finished. Once you wake up from sleeping off your all-nighter, here are some ideas so that next time, you can get your paper done weeks ahead of time and can do your own thing instead of panicking the night before!

Learn from Improv Greats

I hate to break this to you, but improvisational comedians don't really come up with everything on the spot. They usually have a few "canned" segments that they weave into the contexts that arise. Similarly, you should have a few topics of interest. Ideally, you should pick these off the syllabus the moment you get it, do reading assignments with an eye towards them, and keep working with these ideas (though obviously, do not re-use a paper) in your classes. If you go to a school that requires a thesis or capstone to graduate, you'll be doing yourself a favor. If you don't, you'll still make your life a lot easier, and hopefully find a way to learn something you care about. If you give yourself a few "expert topics," you'll be working smarter, not harder, and best of all, find a way to make even the stuff that seems useless work for you. "Adopt" a topic and work with and from it for each class.

Here's a few examples.

Please note*: I used a random name generator (*BehindTheName.com*) for each of these names, so for heaven's sake, don't read any ethnicity or gender stuff into the scenarios.*

Paul is considering grad school for psychology and loves all his psych courses. He has to take an art history class this term. Even though everyone knows Freudian psychology is complete bullshit, you can't deny its importance, so he plans to write a final paper on Freudian symbolism in twentieth century art. This strategy lets him build bridges between a class he doesn't really love and some courses that he's really passionate about. He has picked an angle he already knows something about, and he is finding a way to make the class useful to him.

Parvati is pretty passionate about the issue of for-profit prisons (alliteration is unintentional, I swear). She volunteers with a group on campus that opposes for-profit prisons, and she helps collect books to send to prisoners. Her major is math, however, and even though she cares a lot about society, she isn't too interested in her sociology class, nor is she interested in majoring in it. However, she has to write a paper for her required Intro to Sociology course. You know what she's going to pick! But let's say Parvati also has an English class that she's a little behind in because of her demanding Calc class. She could write about prisons in the books on the syllabus (literal or figurative prisons), or about the role of for-profit institutions in society. She could write about the novels *Crime and Punishment* or *Alias Grace*. In a business class, she could argue that these businesses operate on a flawed model.

Last semester, **Marti** worked on a team presentation for speech class that introduced the issue of foster children who end up becoming drug users. This semester, she is in **Paul's** developmental psych class, and it's not especially her jam; she likes programming and coding a lot more than psychology. However, she decides she's going to write the term paper on attachment styles and foster children. She already has a few sources from the presentation last term, so she's off to a running start on an excellent literature review, thus saving her time to develop the next big app (maybe one that helps foster kids somehow?).

Sofia has a big interest in World War II because her grandmother was a Holocaust survivor. She's a pre-med major, but she decides early on that she's going to **write what she knows** for every class in which a paper is required and in which she has the opportunity to pick her topic. English lit? She writes about *Maus* or one of the many high-quality Holocaust novels. Psychology? She investigates trauma, especially among Holocaust survivors. Sociology? She focuses on the American home front efforts during the war. For her neuro specialty classes, she focuses on geriatrics and Holocaust survivors.

Anne cares about recycling and wants to go into waste management (No, not the kind from *The Sopranos*). Her roommate, **Sofia**, gave her the idea to **write what she knows**, and she sticks with it for all of undergrad as she pursues a degree in chemistry. For psychology class, she researches attitudes about recycling and conducts an online survey assessing people's attitudes and reactions to different recycling slogans. In English class, she researches eco-writing and the creative writing that has come out of conservation. For composition class, she writes a five-page paper passionately arguing for improved recycling facilities at her school's campus. She writes a film paper on *An Inconvenient Truth*.

Obviously, not everyone will have the opportunity to pick their topics for every paper, but you can find an *angle* that you can use repeatedly in many different assignments. For Paul, it might be psychology. For Parvati, it might be social justice and power. For Marti, it could be helping disadvantaged children. For Sofia, it might be preserving the memories of the Holocaust or, more broadly, helping people with trauma. For Anne, it could be implementing better resource management. All of these people are working smarter, not harder, because they are building a focused research library for future assignments.

You don't have to do this with broad topics or specific causes, too. Let's say you find a specific school of thought in an intro philosophy class that you like (or at least that you remember). Try applying that type of analysis to future papers: Utilitarianism can be a "lens" through which to evaluate social policy, literature, film, and so on.

Read, read, read

You might hate this part. Most people do. But the best way to get better at writing is to read, read, read. Not just the things you agree with, not just Instagram captions, but *ideas*. Read a wide and diverse variety of formats and authors. Every time you come across something you find interesting, or even outright wrong but worth arguing about, add it to your Mendeley (Or Zotero, or EndNote, or whatever) library. One site I particularly like for thoughtful, challenging articles is ALDaily.com, and Medium.com is emerging as a great site with some intelligent writing. Find a few topics you care about and follow them on Medium, or read the recommended articles on Medium's front page. You should also read the opinion columns from a high-quality newspaper. Some suggestions are *The New York Times, The Washington Post, The Wall Street Journal, Chicago Sun-Times*, and so on.

Read books, too. For new and recent book suggestions, try the *New York Times*' Best Books of (whatever year), or some of the lists on The Millions. For classics, here are a few search suggestions: "10 must-read books for college grads," "best books by people of color," or "Top 20 nearly forgotten classics." Like you hopefully do with your diet, read broadly. And don't spend too much time prevaricating over what to read. Just pick up a book and start.

Vocabulary

There are lots of apps out there, and just as many word-a-day calendars, websites, and so on. I won't bore you with a list (though as always, I'd love to hear your suggestions on social media!). However, find something to continually improve your vocabulary and stick with it. The best defense is a good offense, and they say the pen is mightier than the sword, so assemble yourself a veritable quiver of words. If you can't blind them with brilliance, baffle them with bullshit, and that is *far* easier when you have a wide-ranging vocabulary at your disposal. Trust me…I would know.

Templates

By now, you know how I feel about the formatting fetish that far too many professors seem to have. I will be uploading my website with downloadable templates for APA, Chicago, MLA, and more. With these download-and-go templates, you'll have to worry less about formatting. Check back on my site, Deleuzienne.com!

CHAPTER 6

Pep Talk

I know how you feel. I promise. I have taken on lots of crazy projects with only a few hours to spare, and I have definitely had moments where I thought, "This is impossible and crazy. How can I do this?" You might feel the same way. As Benjamin Spock put it in a famous 1950s parenting book, you know more than you think you do. On nights when I'm facing down enormous deadlines, I usually chant stupid things to myself, like, "You CAN you MUST you SHOULD and you WILL!" It just makes the dog look at me funny, but I think there's something to telling yourself a few positive things. Hence, I'm going to tell you a few positive things, because in my experience, chances are that not a lot of professors or teachers have done so. But first, let's talk pessimism.

Worst case scenarios

Unfortunately, far too often as a professor and as a writer, I have worked with poor souls who feel that their world will *absolutely end* if they get a bad grade. They're worried about really valid concerns like getting dropped from teams or losing scholarships. I know that failure can feel absolutely devastating, and believe it or not, I have done more than my fair share of it myself.

> **For that reason, if you are feeling that your life absolutely hinges on a grade (or anything else), I urge you to call a hotline.** In the U.S. (and, as far as I can tell, in Canada as well), the confidential National Suicide Prevention Lifeline is **1-800-273-8255** and even has an online chat feature. In the United Kingdom, Samaritans is also 24/7 and can be reached at **116 123** (in both the U.K. and the ROI).
>
> Even if you fail an entire class, **nothing is worth ending your life over, or even considering it**.

Part of the long, sad process of becoming an adult is realizing that you are going to fail at some things, whether it is a class you struggle with, a romantic interest, or assembling IKEA furniture. I like to think I am a full-fledged, semi-successful grown-up, but I personally have failed at endless dates and relationships, completing creative projects, gym-related New Year's Resolutions, academic pursuits, keeping a sickly foster kitten alive for more than 18 hours, my PhD exams the first go, my driver's license test the first time, one quarter of chemistry class in high school, remembering to pay the trash bill on time this past month, calling my great-aunt to say happy birthday before she died, and getting around to visiting my father before he died. And that is just the list of things I personally consider myself as having failed at. I am sure my exes and former professors could gleefully add to this.

Writing out that list stings, but it's no better or worse than anyone else's. And every time one of these paralyzing things happened, the rest of the world went on. Once, after a particularly bad dating failure, a good friend took me on a drive around the natural areas of our state. We stopped at a waterfall. This friend said to me, and this is an exact quote, "This waterfall has been here for 10,000 years. It'll still be here whether you are dating someone or not, or whether you have student loans or not."

When you feel that it's totalizing, or that you have truly screwed up your life beyond repair, try to go out in public or in nature. Put it in perspective a little. Do some exercise. Go somewhere where you will be around people, but not necessarily have to interact with them (a park, a big student center, a gym). Life goes on. Sometimes that's beautiful and sometimes that's cruel. Sometimes failure happens, but how you choose to respond to it and to integrate it into your life story is up to you.

OK, that was enough depressing talk about failure!

QUICK TIP:

*Sometimes an F is not even the end of the road. Often, your professor is happy to meet with you and discuss the reasons for a grade. The syllabus will likely outline options for grade appeals. **If you think your professor has graded you truly unfairly, consider meeting with the course director, department chair, or even the dean**. There may be options to remedy disappointing grades, and I encourage you to be proactive. Meet with your professor and ask what you can do to remedy it (not whether you can). Some will offer a resubmission opportunity, or extra credit assignments.*

All that being said, here are four things to keep in mind:

The perfect is the enemy of the good, and don't try to reinvent the wheel

This sounds like something a grandparent might say, but it is true. These two adages are related, so I put them together here in this section. A common coping strategy for anxiety is to fuss at things, especially projects, endlessly to just avoid letting go. And why not? You tell yourself you have high standards, that you're a perfectionist, and that you want it to be just right. But at a certain point it might be worth asking yourself if this type of perfectionism is not just trying to control the situation in disguise. With a paper, you have to let it go and let someone else judge it. And that's very frightening.

However, even if it's not perfect, your obsession with producing something perfect could be preventing you from turning in something perfectly *good*. It is better for you that your five-page paper on *Macbeth* meet the requirements and be handed in than that you try to reinvent the field of Shakespearean criticism. One of the most unfair things about contemporary education is that creativity and innovation are not rewarded, especially at the undergraduate level. Unfortunately, you are supposed to just meet the requirements, presumably as preparation for your career in middle management. The frustration from that dynamic has driven many hundreds of students to my services over the years.

Take your brilliant and creative ideas and do something else with them! Remember the concept of the "text pasture." If you think you have something unique to say that doesn't fit in the paper, start a blog or even just try to chat with your professor about it during their office hours.

Something is better than nothing

With extremely rare exception, I would much prefer that students hand in a completely terrible paper rather than just nothing. Even if you pound out something average or below-average the night before, that's still way better than shrugging and offering a lame excuse. And as I have been saying, you probably know more than you think you do. You are your own worst critic, and whatever you write is probably not going to be the worst thing your professor has ever read or seen in their life. When I was teaching (a certain course I shall not name here), the official policy from the course director was that if a student even handed in a paper that so much as vaguely met the page count, and if it was not blatantly plagiarized, the minimum grade we could give was a D-. So, you might be surprised.

Work Smarter, Not Harder

I hope you haven't been doing shots every time I've said that in this book, because you will have a nasty hangover. Regardless, it's an important mantra. Working harder is not necessarily working more efficiently. It's worth it to invest a little time in developing a system to save you time on something later on. That is working smarter, not harder. Always look for ways to save yourself time later, whether that means writing a paper about a topic you already know a lot about, defining AutoCorrects in MS Word (Seriously, my AutoCorrects file is like 18 MB now, much to the shock of the very nice online chat help guy who helped me migrate it to a new computer recently!), or using the super-powers of a citation generator. Every time will get easier.

YOU <u>CAN</u> DO IT. NOW GO DO IT!

ABOUT THE AUTHOR

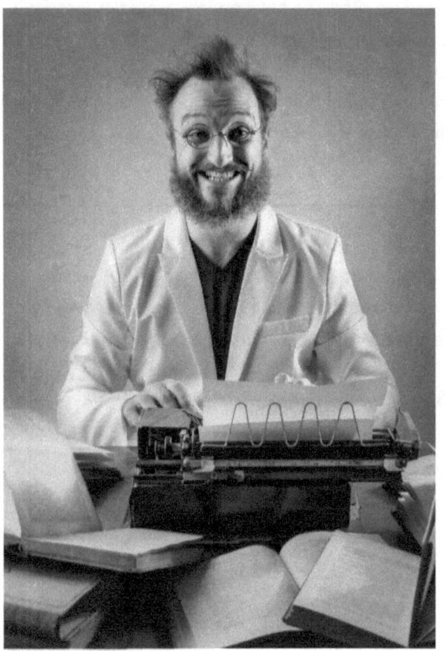

Deleuzienne is a writer who lives somewhere in the United States. This is not actually a picture of Deleuzienne. It is a stock photo of a random stock photo guy. Have you ever wondered about the people who become stock photo people, like the person who is actually pictured in this image? Deleuzienne does. Anyway, check out http://deleuzienne.com/ for exclusive information about forthcoming eBooks, exclusive templates, and other resources to help students!

www.ingramcontent.com/pod-product-compliance
Lightning Source LLC
Chambersburg PA
CBHW031434250726
48656CB00002B/980